Koh Samui (Thailand) Travel Guide 2023-2024

Koh Samui: Island Paradise in the Heart of Europe

Agatha Josiane

Copyright © 2023 by Agatha Josiane

Table of Contents

Chapter 1: Introduction to Koh Samui

1.1 Overview of Koh Samui

Koh Samui is a tropical paradise tucked in the Gulf of Thailand. It is the second-largest island in Thailand and has become one of the country's most famous tourist destinations. Known for its magnificent white sandy beaches, crystal-clear waters, and lush green environs, Koh Samui presents a perfect blend of natural beauty, lively culture, and fine amenities.

The island attracts a broad mix of people, from newlyweds seeking romance to adrenaline junkies eager for spectacular water sports. With its comfortable atmosphere throughout the year, Koh Samui provides a retreat for sun-seekers and beach fans. It boasts a laid-back environment that invites visitors who seek to escape the stress and bustle of everyday life and immerse themselves in a tranquil and refreshing setting.

1.2 History of Koh Samui

Koh Samui has a rich and interesting history that extends back over 1,200 years. Originally occupied by fishermen and maritime merchants, the island has experienced the influences of numerous civilizations, including Chinese, Malay, and Indian. It was an important economic city in the 17th century, luring traders from neighboring countries.

In the late 19th century, Koh Samui became famous for its flourishing coconut commerce, with vast plantations across the island. The coconuts were a vital source of income for the locals, and their products, such as coconut oil and copra, were shipped to other areas of the globe.

In the 1970s, Koh Samui evolved as tourists recognized its natural beauty and began to explore the island. This marked the beginning of the tourism industry on the island, and since then, it has flourished tremendously, drawing visitors from all parts of the world.

1.3 Geographical Features

Koh Samui is characterized by its distinct geographical characteristics that contribute to its magnificent natural beauty. The island has an area of around 228 square kilometers and is surrounded by more than 80 smaller islands. It is part of the Chumphon Archipelago and is roughly 35 kilometers northeast of Surat Thani, the closest mainland city.

The island's coastline spans around 50 kilometers and is flanked by magnificent beaches. From the bustling and colorful Chaweng Beach to the more tranquil and beautiful beaches like Maenam and Lipa Noi, each delivers a different experience to travelers. The pure blue waters surrounding the island are perfect for swimming, snorkeling, and diving, with a profusion of vivid marine life and dazzling coral reefs.

Inland, Koh Samui is bordered by magnificent tropical rainforests, gorgeous coconut plantations, and rolling hills. The highest point on the island is Khao Pom, reaching a height of roughly 635 meters. The interior is dotted with waterfalls, such as Na Muang and Hin Lad, where guests may cool themselves and admire the natural beauty of the island.

Koh Samui is also famous for its odd rock formations, including the legendary Grandmother and Grandfather Rocks (Hin Ta and Hin Yai), which imitate male and female genitalia. These unusual landmarks have become big tourist attractions and are generally related to local folklore.

Overall, the geography of Koh Samui provides a breathtaking landscape that includes pristine beaches, thick woodlands, and interesting natural treasures, making it a superb resort.

Chapter 2: Planning Your Trip

2.1 Best Time to Visit

Koh Samui is equipped with a tropical climate that gives pleasant temperatures and sufficient sunlight throughout the year. However, it's vital to consider the weather patterns and tourist seasons when preparing for your holiday.

The peak season in Koh Samui generally arrives between December and February when the weather is delightfully dry and temperatures range from 25°C to 30°C (77°F to 86°F). This season draws a considerable number of tourists, hence hotel costs tend to be higher. It's advisable to schedule reservations well in advance if you intend to come during this season.

The shoulder season, from March to May, can be a good time to visit because the people thin out, and prices are substantially cheaper. However, the temperature and humidity levels soar, with sporadic showers. June through

October is the low season, defined by increasing rains and occasional storms, but it may also be a good time to find deals on hotels and fewer people.

2.2 Duration of Stay

The suitable length of your stay in Koh Samui primarily hinges on your interests and the activities you wish to participate. To enjoy the island's magnificence and see its key attractions properly, a minimum of four to five days is suggested. This allows ample time to relax on the beaches, view cultural sites, and participate in water sports or other excursions.

If you're planning to integrate island hopping or exploring surrounding destinations such as Koh Phangan or Koh Tao, consider extending your stay to a week or more. This gives you a more detailed study of the area and the chance to immerse yourself in the island's special charm.

2.3 Budgeting and Expenses

Budgeting for your holiday to Koh Samui entails considering various things, including hotel, transportation, food, activities, and shopping. Here's a breakdown of the key expenses:

Accommodation: Koh Samui has a range of accommodations to suit various budgets. Luxury resorts and coastal villas may be rather pricy, but mid-range hotels and guesthouses provide more cheap alternatives. Budget-friendly hotels, such as hostels and guesthouses, are also available.

Transportation: Getting around the island is very basic and affordable. Renting a scooter or automobile is a popular choice for sightseeing at your leisure, with rental costs ranging from 200 to 800 Thai Baht per day. Taxis and Songthaews (shared pick-up cars) are also available, with charges changing depending on the distance.

Meals: Koh Samui offers a booming culinary scene, giving a broad range of dining choices to suit diverse budgets. Local Thai eateries and street food stalls serve affordable and great meals, while luxury restaurants and coastal dining venues offer a more sumptuous eating experience.

Activities: The cost of activities in Koh Samui varies depending on the type of experience you're seeking. trips, such as island hopping trips and snorkeling adventures, may range from 1,000 to 3,000 Thai Baht per person. Entrance fees to landmarks and cultural organizations are quite affordable, with charges frequently ranging from 100 to 500 Thai Baht.

Shopping: Koh Samui is famous for its markets and shopping alternatives. Whether you're searching for local handicrafts, clothes, or souvenirs, there are choices available for every budget. Bargaining is frequent at markets, so be prepared to bargain for the best cost.

2.4 Visa and Entry Requirements

Before traveling to Koh Samui, it's necessary to acquaint yourself with the visa and admission requirements for Thailand. The precise requirements may vary dependent on your nationality. Here are some general guidelines:

Visa Exemption: Citizens of various countries are eligible for visa exemption, enabling them to visit Thailand without a visa for a certain duration (typically 30 days). However, it's vital to verify whether your country is qualified for this exemption and ensure that your passport has at least six months of validity remaining.

Visa-on-Arrival: Some countries may be eligible for a visa-on-arrival, which authorizes a stay of up to 15 days. This option requires you to apply for the visa upon arrival at the relevant immigration checkpoints in Thailand.

Tourist Visa: If you plan to stay in Thailand for the long term or your nation is not eligible for visa exemption or visa-on-arrival, you may need to apply for a tourist visa in advance from a Thai embassy or consulate in your home country. The tourist visa typically enables a stay of up to 60 days, with the opportunity of extending it once inside Thailand.

It's best to consult the official website of the Thai embassy or consulate in your country for the most up-to-date and precise information on visa requirements.

2.5 Travel Insurance

Obtaining travel insurance is essential advisable when visiting Koh Samui or any abroad area. Travel insurance offers coverage for unanticipated scenarios such as medical emergencies, travel cancellations or delays, lost or stolen items, and personal responsibility.

When obtaining travel insurance, consider the following factors:

Medical Coverage: Ensure that the insurance policy covers adequate coverage for medical costs, including hospitalization, emergency medical evacuation, and repatriation.

vacation Cancellation/Interruption: Look for coverage that protects your investment in case your vacation has to be canceled or cut short due to unexpected reasons such as sickness, accident, or natural calamities.

Lost or Stolen items: Choose a policy that covers coverage for lost or stolen baggage, personal goods, or travel documentation like passports or visas.

Adventure Activities: If you wish to partake in adventurous activities such as diving or zip-lining, check that your insurance coverage includes these activities and any associated dangers.

Read the insurance terms and conditions carefully to understand the coverage restrictions, exclusions, and claim procedures. It's crucial to purchase travel insurance as soon as you arrange your trip to ensure you're protected from the minute you start your holiday.

Remember to carry a copy of your travel insurance policy and emergency contact information with you during your holiday to Koh Samui.

By considering the optimal time to visit, length of stay, budgeting and expenses, visa and admission requirements, and getting travel insurance, you can correctly plan your trip to Koh Samui and ensure a smooth and pleasurable travel experience.

Chapter 3: Getting to Koh Samui

Koh Samui, an excellent island situated in the Gulf of Thailand, is a famous tourist destination recognized for its pristine beaches, vibrant culture, and amazing natural beauty. To make your journey to Koh Samui straightforward and hassle-free, it's vital to have a complete grasp of the different transportation possibilities accessible. This chapter will provide you with complete information regarding flights to Koh Samui, ferry services, and transportation on the island.

3.1 Flights to Koh Samui

Koh Samui has an international airport, Samui International Airport (USM), which is well-connected to major cities in Thailand and numerous foreign destinations. The airport is located on the northeastern side of the island, around 2 kilometers from the main tourist destination of Chaweng Beach.

When preparing for your holiday to Koh Samui, consider the following concerns relating to flights:

3.1.1 Airlines and Routes

Several local and international airlines operate regular flights to Samui International Airport. Thai Airways, Bangkok Airways, and AirAsia are among the main carriers serving Koh Samui. Direct flights are available from Bangkok, Phuket, Krabi, Chiang Mai, Singapore, Hong Kong, Kuala Lumpur, and other regional hubs.

3.1.2 Flight length

The flight length to Koh Samui varies dependent on the departure point. From Bangkok, the travel takes around 1 hour and 10 minutes, while flights from Singapore and Kuala Lumpur generally take approximately 1 hour and 45 minutes.

3.1.3 Airport Facilities

Samui International Airport provides modern facilities and amenities to assure a pleasant travel experience. These include duty-free boutiques, cafés, currency exchange offices, vehicle rental services, and lounges for affluent tourists.

3.1.4 Airport Transfer

Upon arrival at Samui International Airport, you may conveniently pick transportation solutions for your hotel. Taxis and private transports are available outside the terminal, or you may pre-arrange transportation with your hotel or resort. Additionally, many motor rental organizations operate inside the airport facilities.

3.2 Ferry Services

If you prefer a beautiful route or if you are going from adjacent islands or mainland Thailand, ferry services are a practical and pleasant means of traveling to Koh Samui. The island is well-connected by boats, and different ports serve as departure points.

Consider the following facts while planning your vacation by ferry:

3.2.1 Ferry companies

There are numerous ferry companies offering services to Koh Samui. Raja Ferry, Seatran Discovery, and Lomprayah are among the well-known firms operating both passenger and automotive ferry services. These operators provide several departure destinations, including Surat Thani, Koh Phangan, and Koh Tao.

3.2.2 Ferry Routes and Duration

The most regular ferry routes to Koh Samui are from Surat Thani, Koh Phangan, and Koh Tao. The length of the cruise depends on the departure point and the sort of boat. From Surat Thani, the boat ride takes around 1.5 to 2 hours, but, from Koh Phangan and Koh Tao, it generally takes around 30 minutes to 1 hour.

3.2.3 Ferry amenities

Most boats operating in Koh Samui are well-equipped with comfortable seats, onboard restrooms, and refreshment amenities. Some boats also offer air-conditioned seating areas and outdoor decks, enabling guests to enjoy magnificent views throughout the journey.

3.2.4 Ticket Booking

It is advisable to book your ferry tickets in advance, particularly during peak tourist seasons, to ensure availability. Tickets may be bought online on the boat operators' official websites or at recognized ticketing booths. It's advised to arrive at the port at least 30 minutes before the specified departure time.

3.3 Transportation on the Island

Once you arrive in Koh Samui, there are numerous transportation possibilities to visit the island and move around conveniently. Consider the following types of transportation available:

3.3.1 Taxis

Taxis are generally accessible in Koh Samui, and they are a useful solution for short distances or when traveling with heavy baggage. Taxis operate on predetermined costs or metered rates, depending on the style of taxi. Make sure to negotiate the charge or confirm the usage of the meter before starting your travel.

3.3.2 Songthaews

Songthaews are open-air customized pickup trucks with bench seats at the rear. They are a popular and economical form of transportation for both locals and tourists. Songthaews follow set routes over the island and may be hailed along the major highways. They generally work on a shared basis, and the charge is paid upon reaching the destination.

3.3.3 Motorbike and Car Rentals

Renting a motorbike or a car is a popular solution for individuals who prefer independence and flexibility while visiting Koh

Samui. Several rental organizations give a comprehensive assortment of vehicles, including scooters, motorcycles, sedans, and jeeps. However, it is necessary to have a valid driver's license and be versed in local traffic laws and regulations.

3.3.4 Bicycle Rentals

For persons who like a slower pace and wish to explore the island at their leisure, bicycle rentals are given in numerous regions. Riding a bicycle around Koh Samui enables you to unearth hidden pearls, enjoy stunning coastal routes, and immerse yourself in the island's grandeur.

3.3.5 Walking

Koh Samui's small size and pedestrian-friendly districts make walking a practical alternative, especially in bustling cities like Chaweng and Bophut. Walking not only enables you to enjoy the island's ambiance but also encourages you to visit local businesses, markets, and attractions along the path.

Understanding the transportation methods available to reach Koh Samui and move about the island helps guarantee a smooth and enjoyable travel experience. Whether you choose to fly, take a boat, or utilize local transportation, you'll have the freedom to explore all the beautiful sites and immerse yourself in the unique culture that Koh Samui has to offer.

Chapter 4: Accommodation Options

Koh Samui has a broad array of hotel solutions to fit every traveler's preferences and budget. Whether you're seeking lavish resorts, mid-range hotels and villas, budget-friendly accommodations, or unconventional stays at eco-resorts, the island offers it all. This chapter will walk you through the numerous kinds of lodgings available, offering you complete information to aid you make an educated pick for your stay in Koh Samui.

4.1 Luxury Resorts and Hotels

Koh Samui is famous for its spectacular resorts and hotels that offer world-class amenities and great service. These enterprises give a superb blend of comfort, elegance, and magnificent natural beauty. The island offers various worldwide acclaimed resorts, such as the Four Seasons Resort Koh Samui, Banyan Tree Samui, and Six Senses Samui, each giving a different and beautiful experience.

Luxury resorts in Koh Samui usually include individual villas with spectacular ocean views, private pools, and direct beach access. They give a large array of amenities including spa and wellness facilities, gourmet dining restaurants, seaside bars, workout centers, and recreational activities. Impeccable service and attention to detail are the features of these hotels, providing a delightful and memorable stay for visitors.

4.2 Mid-range Hotels and Villas

For travelers seeking good housing without breaking the budget, Koh Samui offers a variety of mid-range hotels and villas. These options offer a blend between affordability and quality, making them popular among families, couples, and budget-conscious travelers.

Mid-range hotels on Koh Samui feature big rooms or bungalows with vital conveniences like air conditioning, Wi-Fi, and private bathrooms. Many of these hotels provide swimming pools, on-site cafés, and tour help to enrich your stay. Some popular mid-range choices include Ibis Samui Bophut, Chaweng Regent Beach Resort, and Amari Koh Samui.

Alternatively, if you want more privacy and space, you may consider a mid-range villa rental. These villas often come with many bedrooms, a fully supplied kitchen, a private pool, and outdoor living areas. They are perfect for families or groups of friends seeking a self-catering accommodation alternative. Websites like Airbnb and Booking.com give a vast range of mid-priced villas to choose from.

4.3 Budget-friendly Accommodations

Travelers on a restricted budget may locate dozens of wallet-friendly hotels on Koh Samui. These solutions deliver low rates without compromising comfort or convenience. From guesthouses and hostels to budget hotels, there are various possibilities accessible for individuals looking to save money on housing.

Guesthouses and hostels are popular among backpackers and lonely travelers, providing common dormitories or private rooms at affordable pricing. These establishments usually have public spaces where guests may socialize and discuss trip experiences. Some suggested budget-friendly choices are Samui Verticolor, Lub ba Koh Samui Chaweng Beach, and Bondi Hotel Samui.

Budget hotels are another possibility for cost-conscious tourists. While they may not provide the same degree of luxury as high-end resorts, they supply clean and comfortable rooms with the essential comforts. The expenses are frequently more reasonable, making them excellent for travelers who wish to spend their income on seeing the island rather than on accommodation. Examples of affordable hotels on Koh Samui include Ploen Chaweng Koh Samui, Chaweng Park Place, and Samui Pier Beach Front & Resort.

4.4 Unique Stays and Eco-Resorts

For those wishing for a more unique and sustainable hotel experience, Koh Samui offers a selection of eco-resorts and atypical stays.

These choices enable you to engage with nature, support environmentally responsible techniques, and immerse yourself in the island's distinctive ambiance.

Eco-resorts in Koh Samui concentrate on reducing their environmental influence through varied measures including solar power, water conservation, and organic farming. These resorts typically combine well with their natural surroundings, providing eco-friendly accommodation in the style of bamboo bungalows, treehouses, or coastal eco-villas. Some prominent eco-resorts on the island include Tongsai Bay, Samui Eco Resort, and X2 Koh Samui Resort - All Spa Inclusive.

In addition to eco-resorts, Koh Samui also has unique lodgings that cater to certain interests or themes. This contains seaside glamping spots, traditional Thai-style homestays, or rustic beach cottages. These hotels enable the finding of a separate aspect of Koh Samui and offer amazing encounters.

Whether you chose a luxurious resort, a mid-range hotel, a budget-friendly accommodation, or a unique eco-resort, Koh Samui has a vast number of alternatives to satisfy each traveler's preferences. Consider your budget, preferred amenities, and desired experience to pick the ideal hotel for your vacation to this gorgeous Thai island.

Chapter 5: Exploring the Beaches

Koh Samui is famous for its stunning beaches, each having a distinct ambiance and attractions. In this chapter, we will dive into the greatest beaches on the island and present you with an in-depth guide to making the most of your beach-hopping experience.

5.1 Chaweng Beach

Chaweng Beach is the most popular and vibrant beach in Koh Samui. Located on the east shore of the island, it runs across roughly 7 kilometers, with powdery white sand and crystal-clear blue waters. Chaweng Beach is flanked by a multitude of beachfront resorts, restaurants, clubs, and boutiques, making it a popular and vibrant destination.

5.1.1 Water Sports and Activities

Chaweng Beach is famous for adrenaline junkies and water sports aficionados. Enjoy exciting sports such as jet skiing, parasailing, and banana boat excursions. The beach also provides possibilities for snorkeling and scuba diving, enabling you to enjoy the rich marine life and spectacular coral reefs.

5.1.2 Beachfront Dining and Nightlife

Indulge in a large array of dining alternatives along Chaweng Beach, ranging from beachside seafood establishments to international cuisines. As the sun sets, the beach turns into a lively nightlife area, with beach bars and clubs providing live music, DJs, and fire displays.

5.1.3 Shopping and Markets

Chaweng Beach boasts a vibrant shopping scene, with several markets and enterprises supplying garments, accessories, and souvenirs. Don't miss the chance to enjoy the Chaweng Walking Street Night Market, where you may find local handicrafts, street cuisine, and live entertainment.

5.2 Lamai Beach

Situated on the southeast coast of Koh Samui, Lamai Beach is the second-largest and most serene beach on the island. It offers a laid-back vibe, making it a popular option for families and couples seeking tranquillity.

5.2.1 Hin Ta and Hin Yai Rocks

Lamai Beach is noted for its natural beauty, especially the stunning Hin Ta and Hin Yai Rocks, widely known as the Grandfather and Grandmother Rocks. These granite structures replicate male and female genitalia and have become a recognized tourist attraction.

5.2.2 Spa and Wellness Retreats

Lamai Beach is loaded with health centers and spas providing refreshing treatments and traditional Thai massages. Pamper yourself with a spa day or join a yoga class to develop inner peace.

5.2.3 Sunday Night Walking Street

Every Sunday, Lamai Beach comes alive with the busy Sunday Night Walking Street market. Explore the merchants offering local street food, handicrafts, clothes, and souvenirs while enjoying live music performances.

5.3 Bophut Beach

Bophut Beach, situated on the northern side of Koh Samui, is famous for its gorgeous fishing village and wonderful environment. It blends traditional Thai traits with a bohemian flair, making it popular among travelers seeking a special beach experiences.

5.3.1 Fisherman's Village

In the middle of Bophut Beach is the Fisherman's Village, a lovely and atmospheric enclave crammed with boutique boutiques, art galleries, and restaurants. Explore the narrow alleys and absorb the local charm while tasting wonderful seafood at beach cafes.

5.3.2 Wat Bophut

Visit Wat Bophut, a Buddhist temple located near the beach, famous for its brilliant golden Buddha image. Take a minute to immerse yourself in the tranquil setting and observe the gorgeous architecture.

5.3.3 Friday Night Walking Street

Every Friday, Bophut Beach features a lively night market known as the Bophut Walking Street. Immerse yourself in the vibrant ambiance as you browse among the booths featuring local delicacies, handcrafted crafts, and live entertainment.

5.4 Maenam Beach

Maenam Beach is a calm beach situated on the northern coast of Koh Samui. It offers a tranquil sanctuary with its lengthy stretch of white sand and gentle surf, making it a great spot for relaxation and regeneration.

5.4.1 Wat Na Phra Lan

Explore the cultural side of Maenam Beach by visiting Wat Na Phra Lan, a Buddhist temple famous for its stunning golden Buddha image and wonderful artwork. Take a moment for meditation and immerse yourself in the spiritual ambiance.

5.4.2 Maenam Walking Street

Discover the local foods and crafts at the Maenam Walking Street, hosted every Thursday evening. Sample amazing street food, shop for handmade items, and watch live performances exhibiting traditional Thai music and dance.

5.5 Choeng Mon Beach

Located on the northeastern point of Koh Samui, Choeng Mon Beach provides a serene and remote ambiance. The beach is situated in a cove surrounded by lush green hills, creating a great atmosphere for leisure and romance.

5.5.1 Watersports and Snorkeling

Engage in water activities like kayaking and paddleboarding along the calm shores of

Choeng Mon Beach. Explore the colorful underwater world by snorkeling in the clear waters and discovering the vivid coral reefs.

5.5.2 Luxury Resorts and Spas

Choeng Mon Beach is home to some of the most lavish resorts and spas on the island. Indulge in world-class facilities, superb dining experiences, and invigorating spa treatments while enjoying gorgeous ocean views.

5.6 Silver Beach

Tucked away on the eastern coast of Koh Samui, Silver Beach is a hidden treasure noted for its pristine beauty and tranquil environment. With its pure white sand and azure waters, this beach offers a tranquil and romantic getaway.

5.6.1 Relaxation and Sunbathing

Unwind on the soft sand at Silver Beach, bathe in the warm tropical sun, and listen to the peaceful lapping of the waves. The beach's quiet nature offers a fantastic background for sunbathing and relaxation.

5.6.2 Beachfront Restaurants and Bars

Savor tasty meals and cool drinks at the beachfront restaurants and taverns along Silver Beach. Enjoy a romantic meal by the sea or enjoy drinks while witnessing a gorgeous sunset.

5.6.3 Kayaking and Paddleboarding

Explore the lovely waters of Silver Beach by kayaking or paddleboarding. Rent equipment and embark on a quiet tour, seeking secluded coves and enjoying the tranquillity of the surrounding landscape.

By seeing these different and magnificent beaches, you will fully understand the beauty and charm of Koh Samui's coastline. Whether you seek a lively ambiance or a solitary sanctuary, the island presents a range of choices to fit every traveler's taste.

Chapter 6: Island Hopping & Excursions

6.1 Angthong National Marine Park

Angthong National Marine Park is a stunning archipelago of 42 islands situated northwest of Koh Samui. This protected marine park includes an area of roughly 102 square kilometers and is famous for its spectacular limestone cliffs, emerald-green oceans, and spotless white sandy beaches. A day visit to Angthong National Marine Park is a must for nature aficionados and adventure seekers.

6.1.1 Getting to Angthong National Marine Park

To reach Angthong National Marine Park, you may book a tour from Koh Samui that includes transportation by speedboat or traditional long-tail boat. The journey takes around one to two hours, depending on the kind of vessel and weather conditions. Many tour operators give hotel pick-up services that, provide a pleasant and hassle-free experience for tourists.

6.1.2 Exploring the Islands of Angthong National Marine Park

Once you get to Angthong National Marine Park, you'll be surprised by the stunning scenery and the diverse variety of islands to explore. Each island has its distinct charm and offers different activities for holidaymakers. You may enjoy sunbathing on the lovely beaches, discovering hidden lagoons and caverns, or walking to breathtaking overlooks for panoramic views of the surrounding islands. Some of the most popular islands within Angthong National Marine Park include Koh Wua Talap, Koh Mae Ko, and Koh Sam Sao. Koh Wua Talap is the biggest island in the park and acts as the headquarters, supplying amenities like a tourist center, hotels, and camping areas. Koh Mae Ko is noted for its Emerald Lake (known as Talay Nai), a stunning inland saltwater lake surrounded by limestone cliffs. Koh Sam Sao is famous for its gorgeous beaches and bright coral reefs, excellent for snorkeling and diving fanatics.

6.1.3 Snorkeling and Diving in Angthong National Marine Park

The crystal-clear waters of Angthong National Marine Park are teeming with various marine life, making it a treat for snorkelers and divers. The coral reefs surrounding the islands are home to a vast diversity of species, including colorful tropical fish, sea turtles, and even whale sharks if you're fortunate. Snorkeling and diving excursions are often included in the day trips, enabling you to explore the underwater world and appreciate the beauty of the marine fauna.

Snorkeling spots like Koh Wao and Koh Tai Plao provide great clarity and an abundance of marine life. For certified divers, different dive sites in Angthong National Marine Park cater to diverse levels of competence. Exploring the underwater environment here is a fascinating experience, and diving lovers may notice the vibrant coral gardens, and unusual rock formations, and meet varied aquatic animals.

6.1.4 Hiking and Kayaking Opportunities

Angthong National Marine Park is not merely about the beaches and the water. The islands also give fantastic opportunities for trekking and kayaking. The park is home to lush jungles, hidden waterfalls, and fascinating rock formations waiting to be explored. Many tour companies arrange guided hiking treks, leading you through gorgeous pathways that lead to spectacular overlooks across the archipelago.

Kayaking is another popular activity in Angthong National Marine Park, allowing you to kayak through the serene turquoise waters and locate secluded coves, caves, and mangrove forests. Guided kayak tours are available, ensuring your safety and presenting fascinating information about the flora and creatures you see along the path.

6.1.5 Wildlife and Flora in Angthong National Marine Park

Angthong National Aquatic Park is not only a sanctuary for aquatic life but also home to a vast variety of animals and vegetation. The park is a protected area, and efforts have been conducted to safeguard its natural beauty and fauna. While traveling the islands, you may encounter different varieties of birds, monkeys, lizards, and even unique orchids.

The park's rich forests are formed of tropical rainforest vegetation, including towering trees, ferns, and lovely flowers. Take the time to observe the natural beauty around you and immerse yourself in the tranquil and undisturbed environment that Angthong National Marine Park provides.

6.2 Koh Tao and Koh Nang Yuan

Koh Tao and Koh Nang Yuan are two charming islands situated north of Koh Samui and are famous for their wonderful beaches, bright coral reefs, and numerous aquatic life. These islands are renowned among divers and snorkelers owing to their extraordinary underwater purity and rich marine environment.

6.2.1 Getting to Koh Tao and Koh Nang Yuan

To get Koh Tao and Koh Nang Yuan from Koh Samui, you may use a ferry or a speedboat. Several ferry routes operate daily, and the ride generally takes around 1.5 to 2 hours. High-speed catamarans provide a quicker alternative, with voyage durations as short as 1 hour. It's encouraged to book your tickets in advance, particularly during peak seasons, to ensure availability.

6.2.2 Beaches and Water Activities on Koh Tao and Koh Nang Yuan

Koh Tao and Koh Nang Yuan offer some of the most stunning beaches in the Gulf of Thailand. Sairee Beach on Koh Tao is the longest and most popular, featuring silky white beaches and vivid blue oceans. It's a beautiful spot for sunbathing, beach volleyball, or just relaxing with a book. Tanote Bay and Shark Bay are other lovely beaches on the island worth researching.

Koh Nang Yuan, on the other hand, is famous for its peculiar and gorgeous beach construction. Connected by a sandbar, the three little islands of Koh Nang Yuan boast powdery white dunes and crystal-clear oceans. You may swim, snorkel, or just bask in the majesty of this natural wonder.

6.2.3 Diving and Snorkeling at Koh Tao and Koh Nang Yuan

Koh Tao is well considered one of the greatest diving spots in Thailand. With its peaceful oceans, outstanding visibility, and abundance of dive locations, it draws divers from all over the globe. The island has a broad range of diving facilities catering to all levels of expertise, from beginners to experienced divers. Whether you're seeking to become certified or want to explore underwater tunnels and pinnacles, Koh Tao offers something for everyone.

Snorkeling is also a popular hobby near Koh Tao and Koh Nang Yuan. You may rent snorkeling gear or join a guided snorkeling expedition to observe the beautiful coral reefs and meet colorful tropical animals. Japanese Gardens, Mango Bay, and Shark Island are some of the top snorkeling spots in the area.

6.2.4 Hiking and Viewpoints

For those wanting adventure on land, Koh Tao and Koh Nang Yuan give alternatives for trekking and stunning viewpoints. On Koh Tao, you may hike to the island's highest point, Two View Rock, which rewards you with panoramic vistas of the surrounding islands and the sparkling ocean. The trek could be arduous but is well worth the effort.

Koh Nang Yuan also includes a trekking pathway that gets you to a wonderful viewpoint seeing the three islands and the sandbar. As you climb, you'll be treated to awe-inspiring views that give for fantastic picture options.

6.2.5 Sustainable Tourism Efforts on Koh Tao and Koh Nang Yuan

Both Koh Tao and Koh Nang Yuan have adopted efforts to foster sustainable tourism and conserve their sensitive environments. The islands are strongly engaged in coral reef conservation efforts, with several organizations working to repair damaged reefs and educate visitors about ethical diving and snorkeling practices.

Several diving establishments on Koh Tao have incorporated eco-friendly measures, such as reef-safe sunscreen policies, regular beach cleanups, and developing marine conservation awareness. By supporting these sustainable tourism initiatives, travelers may help to the preservation of the islands' natural beauty for future generations.

6.3 Koh Phangan

Koh Phangan is an island situated north of Koh Samui and is famous for its stunning beaches, busy nightlife, and the legendary Full Moon Party. While the Full Moon Party is a significant attraction, Koh Phangan features much more than its party scene. The island features beautiful landscapes, secluded bays, and a laid-back ambiance, making it an ideal destination for relaxation and exploration.

6.3.1 Getting to Koh Phangan

To reach Koh Phangan from Koh Samui, you may board a boat from numerous ports, including Bangrak Pier, Maenam Pier, or Nathon Pier. The travel generally takes around 20-30 minutes by a high-speed boat or 1-2 hours by a traditional ferry, depending on the departure location and sea conditions. It's vital to check the boat times in advance, particularly if you're attending the Full Moon Party or traveling during peak seasons.

6.3.2 Beaches and Water Activities on Koh Phangan

Koh Phangan is equipped with a choice of spectacular beaches, each with its particular attraction. Haad Rin is the most recognized beach on the island, notable for staging the Full Moon Party. It's a vibrant and thrilling beach where you may dance the night away under the moonlight. Other popular beaches include Thong Nai Pan, Haad Yao, and Salad Beach, presenting a more relaxed setting and ideal swimming conditions.

Water activities include as snorkeling, kayaking, and paddleboarding are popular around Koh Phangan. You may rent equipment from beachside businesses or join guided tours to explore the hidden coves, coral reefs, and surrounding islands.

6.3.3 Explore the Interior: Waterfalls and Hiking Trails

Koh Phangan's interior is a green wonderland with deep woods, gushing waterfalls, and lovely trekking paths. Take a break from the beaches and experience the island's natural beauty. Phaeng Waterfall is a must-visit, affording a relaxing dip in its natural pools and stunning views from the lookout. Than Sadet Waterfall, Wang Sai Waterfall, and Paradise Waterfall are all worth viewing for their tranquil ambiance and lovely surroundings.

Hiking aficionados may embark on a journey to Khao Ra, the tallest mountain in Koh Phangan. The trek takes you through lush woods and rewards you with panoramic views of the island and nearby islands. It's advisable to hire a local guide to guarantee a safe and happy stay.

6.3.4 Yoga and Wellness Retreats

Koh Phangan has garnered recognition as a venue for yoga and health retreats. The island is loaded with yoga institutions and health resorts creating a calm atmosphere for relaxation and self-discovery. Whether you're a newbie or an experienced practitioner, you may locate a range of yoga classes and seminars catering to various styles and levels.

Many resorts also offer health retreats, detox programs, and spa treatments, enabling you to revitalize your mind, body, and soul. Immerse yourself in the island's tranquil ambiance and experience the holistic lifestyle that Koh Phangan offers.

6.3.5 Authentic Thai Cuisine and Local Culture

Koh Phangan boasts a vast array of eating selections, ranging from modest street food vendors to fancy coastal establishments. You may sample true Thai cuisine, including scrumptious curries, fresh seafood, and aromatic street food delicacies. Don't miss out on eating local favorites like Pad Thai, Tom Yum Goong, and Mango Sticky Rice.

Beyond the culinary pleasures, Koh Phangan also allows the chance to immerse oneself in the local culture. Visit the Thong Sala Night Market to enjoy the vibrant ambiance, sample local cuisines, and shop among handicrafts and souvenirs. You may also explore the island's temples, such as Wat Phu Khao Noi and Wat Nai.

Koh Phangan's traditional festivals, similar to Loy Krathong and Songkran, provide an insight into Thai culture and celebrations. Embrace the celebratory mood and join in these pleasant activities if you have the opportunity.

6.4 Five Islands Tour

The Five Islands Tour is a popular tour from Koh Samui, affording a unique chance to explore a cluster of little islands situated off its southwestern coast. This tour enables you to discover stunning limestone buildings, remote beaches, and colorful aquatic life.

6.4.1 The Five Islands: Koh Tan, Koh Matsum, Koh Taen, Koh Sing, and Koh Si Koh Ha

The Five Islands include Koh Tan, Koh Matsum, Koh Taen, Koh Sing, and Koh Si Koh Ha. Each island has its distinct qualities and provides a unique experience. Koh Tan and Koh Matsum are famous for their shallow coral reefs and are perfect for snorkeling and observing colorful marine life. Koh Taen boasts excellent beaches, while Koh Sing is famous for its green lagoon flanked by limestone cliffs. Koh Si Koh Ha is a secluded island with stunning rock formations and crystal-clear oceans, suitable for swimming and snorkeling.

6.4.2 Snorkeling and Marine Life Encounters

Snorkeling is the highlight of the Five Islands Tour, enabling you to discover the underwater environment and meet a diverse array of marine species. The coral reefs surrounding the islands are home to colorful tropical fish, sea turtles, and various other marine species. Snorkeling equipment is generally supplied as part of the tour package, ensuring that you have everything you need to explore the unique underwater ecosystem.

6.4.3 Beach Picnics and Relaxation

During the Five Islands Tour, you'll have the chance to enjoy beach picnics and relax on stunning shores. The excursion typically includes a stop at a private beach where you may relax, take up the sun, and enjoy a great picnic lunch given by the tour organizer. This tranquil environment enables you to absorb the natural beauty of the islands and create amazing memories.

6.4.4 Mangrove Forest Exploration

One of the unique components of the Five Islands Tour is the possibility to explore the mangrove woodlands that surround Koh Taen. A guided kayak journey through the mangroves enables you to observe the unique habitat up close. Paddle through narrow canals, enjoy the remarkable richness of the mangrove woods, and learn about their ecological worth from professional guides.

6.4.5 Sunset Cruise and Dinner

To complete the Five Islands Tour, some operators give a sunset sail back to Koh Samui, giving a stunning climax to a day of exploration. Enjoy the stunning vistas as the sun sets over the horizon, casting bright hues across the sky. Some tours may include a sunset dinner on board, permitting you to savor a delicious meal while soaking in the beauty of the neighboring islands.

6.5 Sail Rock Diving

Sail Rock, also known as Hin Bai, is a renowned diving location situated between Koh Samui and Koh Phangan. It's recognized as one of the greatest diving locations in the Gulf of Thailand, luring divers from all around the globe. Diving at Sail Rock allows meeting enormous schools of fish, stunning rock formations, and the ability watch the odd vertical swim-through known as the "Chimney."

6.5.1 Sail Rock: Location and Dive Conditions

Sail Rock is situated roughly 15 kilometers northeast of Koh Samui, and it takes around an hour by boat to reach this famed diving destination. The rock erupts from the sea, generating a pinnacle that reaches above the surface and plunges deep into the ocean. The site's location exposes it to strong currents, providing nutrient-rich waters that attract a broad range of marine animals.

Dive conditions at Sail Rock could alter depending on the tides and currents. It's advisable to have some diving skills before trying to dive here because of the possibility of high currents. However, dive operators will offer a detailed briefing and ensure your safety throughout the dive.

6.5.2 Marine Life at Sail Rock

Sail Rock is recognized for its tremendous marine biodiversity, offering a chance to witness a diverse variety of aquatic species. Schools of barracuda, trevally, and snapper are regularly visible spinning around the pinnacle. The region is also frequented by whale sharks during certain seasons of the year, making it an exciting experience for divers fortunate enough to meet them.

Other marine species you may encounter at Sail Rock are angelfish, butterflyfish, moray eels, triggerfish, and anemonefish. The spectacular coral formations, including rainbow soft corals and sea fans, contribute to the visual feast of the dive.

6.5.3 Diving Highlights: The Chimney and Secret Pinnacles

The "Chimney" is one of the distinctive aspects of Sail Rock. This vertical swim-through begins at around 18 meters and continues up to the surface. Divers may enter the chimney and rise via the narrow tunnel, surrounded by intriguing underwater life and brilliant corals. Exiting the chimney at the top provides a wonderful view of the surrounding waterways.

Another highlight of diving at Sail Rock is the Secret Pinnacles. Located slightly away from the main pinnacle, these submerged rocks give a different diving experience. Divers may explore the odd rock formations and uncover a variety of marine animals concealed among the nooks and crevices.

6.5.4 Diving Certifications and Courses

Diving at Sail Rock is perfect for divers of all experience levels, from beginners to advanced. However, due to the site's depth and severe currents, it's advised to have at least an Open

Water certification. If you're a newbie, you may pick a guided dive with an expert instructor who will ensure your safety and take you through the underwater beauty.

For those who desire to develop their diving talents or gain additional certifications, numerous dive schools offer advanced courses, such as the Advanced Open Water Diver and the Deep Diver Specialty, enabling you to explore deeper areas of the site.

6.5.5 Safety and Conservation Efforts

Dive operators at Sail Rock prioritize safety and adhere to severe diving standards. They conduct detailed dive briefings, perform equipment inspections, and ensure divers are completely prepared for the dive. Additionally, dive leaders are knowledgeable about the site's circumstances and marine creatures, further improving the safety and pleasure of the dive.

In terms of conservation efforts, Sail Rock is part of a protected marine environment, and dive firms advise responsible diving activity.

They teach divers about environmental protection, such as maintaining proper buoyancy, not touching or disturbing marine creatures, and avoiding contact with the coral reefs. By practicing ethical diving, tourists may help safeguard the beauty and purity of Sail Rock for future years.

Chapter 7: Cultural and Historical Sites

7.1 Big Buddha Temple (Wat Phra Yai)

The Big Buddha Temple, commonly known as Wat Phra Yai, is one of the most famous structures in Koh Samui. This impressive temple is situated on a tiny island named Koh Faan, linked to the main island by a bridge. The centerpiece of this temple is a towering golden statue of Lord Buddha, which rises at an astonishing height of 12 meters. The Big Buddha statue is visible from many kilometers away and is a symbol of calm, tranquility, and spiritual enlightenment.

As you approach the temple, you'll be met with a majestic stairway lined by mythological snake sculptures called Nagas. Climbing the stairs, you'll experience a feeling of expectancy and respect. Once you reach the summit, the beautiful view of the surrounding region and the great ocean will capture you.

Within the temple grounds, you'll discover various smaller sculptures, shrines, and prayer rooms. These temples are embellished with beautiful decorations and give an insight into Thai Buddhist art and architecture. The temple complex also has a busy marketplace where you may buy religious relics, souvenirs, and traditional Thai handicrafts.

7.2 Wat Plai Laem

Located in the northeast of Koh Samui, Wat Plai Laem is a visually spectacular temple complex that shows a combination of Chinese and Thai architectural traditions. The major feature of this temple is the gigantic figure of the 18-armed Goddess of Mercy, Guanyin. Standing tall and encircled by a lotus pond, the monument is a magnificent sight to see.

As you visit the temple grounds, you'll find exquisite paintings illustrating Buddhist teachings and legends. The rich colors and exquisite artwork create a mesmerizing ambiance. Adjacent to the main temple, you'll discover smaller shrines devoted to different deities and celestial creatures, such as the Laughing Buddha and the Tiger God.

Wat Plai Laem is not merely a place of worship but also a cultural and educational center. It provides visitors a chance to learn about Buddhism, Thai customs, and the value of spiritual activities. If you're fortunate, you may even observe a religious ritual or engage in meditation sessions led by the local monks.

7.3 Wat Khunaram

Wat Khunaram is a remarkable temple notable for its mummified monk, Luang Pho Daeng. The mummified corpse of the respected monk, who died away in 1973, is exhibited in a glass cabinet inside the monastery grounds. Despite being dead for many decades, the monk's corpse displays relatively minor symptoms of deterioration, making it an important spiritual and cultural attraction for the island.

The temple grounds of Wat Khunaram are quiet and serene, giving a pleasant place for introspection and thought. Visitors may pay their respects to Luang Pho Daeng and learn about his life and teachings via educational exhibits and images.

Apart from the mummified monk, Wat Khunaram also has traditional Buddhist structures and magnificent grounds. The mood is one of awe and respect, as residents and visitors alike come to seek blessings and spiritual direction.

7.4 Secret Buddha Garden

Hidden away in the hills of Koh Samui's interior, the Secret Buddha Garden, also known as Magic Garden or Heaven's Garden, is a hidden jewel waiting to be found. Created by a local fruit farmer called Nim Thongsuk, the garden features a collection of sculptures symbolizing different deities, animals, and legendary creatures from Thai mythology.

To reach the Secret Buddha Garden, you'll go on a picturesque trek via lush woods and meandering roads. The garden itself is situated within deep foliage, providing a private and lovely ambiance. As you travel through the paths, you'll see exquisite statues of Buddha, deities, and even comical animals like monkeys and elephants.

Each statue inside the Secret Buddha Garden tells a tale, representing the rich cultural and spiritual legacy of Thailand. The attention to detail and the tranquil atmosphere make this garden an ideal spot for reflection and meditation.

7.5 Hin Ta and Hin Yai Rocks

Hin Ta and Hin Yai, popularly known as the Grandfather and Grandmother Rocks, are natural rock formations found on the southeastern shore of Koh Samui. These unusual formations bore a remarkable similarity to male and female genitalia, and their distinctive shape has become a major tourist attraction and a symbol of fertility.

Legend has it that an old couple was shipwrecked in the region, and their souls changed into rocks as a symbol of everlasting love and oneness. Today, the rocks are considered holy and are thought to bring good fortune to individuals seeking fertility and marital joy.

The rocks are surrounded by spectacular coastal landscapes, affording tourists breathtaking views of the turquoise ocean and white sandy beaches. Nearby, you'll discover stores offering souvenirs and local handicrafts, as well as cafés where you can have a cool drink while taking in the beauty of the shoreline.

Visiting Hin Ta and Hin Yai is not only an opportunity to view an uncommon geological structure but also a chance to dig into local mythology and embrace the cultural beliefs of the island.

Chapter 8: Outdoor Activities

Koh Samui provides a wealth of outdoor activities that appeal to any adventurer's aspirations. Whether you are seeking underwater exploration, adrenaline-pumping sports, or immersive rainforest experiences, this chapter will lead you through the interesting outdoor activities offered on the island.

8.1 Snorkeling and Diving

Koh Samui is surrounded by crystal-clear seas rich with vivid marine life, making it a sanctuary for snorkeling and diving lovers. Embark on a tour to see the underwater treasures of the Gulf of Thailand, where vibrant coral reefs and various marine animals await. Popular snorkeling and diving destinations include Koh Tan, Koh Tao, and Sail Rock.

8.2 Water Sports

For those seeking thrill on the sea's surface, Koh Samui provides a broad choice of water sports activities. Jet skiing, parasailing, kayaking, and paddleboarding are just a few activities accessible. Experience the exhilaration of gliding over the waves or soaring above the blue water while taking in the gorgeous coastline panorama.

8.3 Hiking and Jungle Trekking

Immerse yourself in the gorgeous tropical rainforests of Koh Samui via hiking and jungle trekking excursions. Explore the island's secret pathways, gushing waterfalls, and unusual flora and animals. Popular hiking spots include Na Muang Waterfall, Hin Lad Waterfall, and Khao Pom Viewpoint. Engage with skilled local guides who can enrich your trip by offering their insights into the island's rich biodiversity.

8.4 Zip-lining Adventures

Embark on an adrenaline-fueled ride through the treetops of Koh Samui's lush rainforests with exhilarating zip-lining activities. Soar over the canopies, experiencing panoramic views of the island's natural sceneries. Feel the thrill of exhilaration as you navigate between platforms, dangling far above the earth. Choose from a range of zip-lining courses that appeal to various skill levels and tastes.

8.5 Elephant Sanctuaries

Koh Samui is home to various elephant sanctuaries that encourage ethical and responsible elephant tourism. Visitors get the chance to engage with these amazing animals in a natural and compassionate atmosphere. Engage in activities such as feeding, bathing, and watching elephants while learning about their conservation and care. By visiting respected sanctuaries, you help the preservation of these gentle giants and promote sustainable methods.

As you engage in these outside activities, it is crucial to consider safety. Ensure that you connect with licensed and trustworthy operators who adhere to stringent safety requirements. Follow guidelines offered by expert guides and instructors to make the most of your excursion while minimizing dangers.

Remember to respect the natural environment and animals throughout your outdoor trips. Take care not to harm the sensitive ecosystems and comply with any recommendations or limits placed in place to safeguard the environment.

Whether you are seeking an adrenaline rush, a quiet meeting with nature, or a mix of both, Koh Samui's outdoor activities will appeal to your preferences. Explore the island's undersea delights, indulge in exhilarating water sports, go on jungle excursions, fly through the trees, and interact responsibly with elephants. These adventures will create lasting memories and improve your connection with the natural beauty of Koh Samui.

Chapter 9: Wellness and Spa Retreats

9.1 Spa & Wellness Facilities

Koh Samui is recognized for its magnificent spa and wellness facilities, providing a broad variety of revitalizing treatments and therapies. These institutions offer a quiet setting where guests may rest and participate in different wellness treatments. From traditional Thai massages to modern holistic treatments, the spa and wellness establishments on the island cater to the different demands of guests seeking physical and emotional renewal.

Traditional Thai Spa: Experience the ancient art of Thai massage at one of the numerous traditional spas on the island. Skilled therapists utilize a mix of acupressure, stretching, and rhythmic movements to relieve tension and restore equilibrium to the body. Traditional Thai spas also provide various treatments such as herbal compress massages, hot stone therapies, and body washes utilizing native herbs and materials.

Luxury Spa Resorts: Koh Samui features various luxury resorts that have world-class spas. These resorts provide a selection of distinctive services, including aromatherapy massages, deep tissue massages, and facials utilizing quality organic products. Guests may enjoy spectacular ocean views, private treatment rooms, and state-of-the-art amenities while immersing themselves in the ultimate spa experience.

Wellness Resorts: Koh Samui is home to various wellness resorts that offer full programs for holistic recovery. These retreats integrate numerous components such as yoga, meditation, detoxification, and nutritious food to improve physical, mental, and spiritual well-being. Guests may engage in daily yoga and meditation classes, get individualized wellness consultations, and luxuriate in delicious meals meant to cleanse and nourish the body.

9.2 Yoga & Meditation Retreats

For those seeking inner calm and spiritual progress, Koh Samui offers a range of yoga and meditation retreats. Surrounded by the island's natural splendor, these retreats give the ideal location to develop your practice and connect with your inner self.

Yoga lessons: Many resorts and health facilities in Koh Samui offer daily yoga lessons for practitioners of all levels. Experienced teachers educate participants through several kinds of yoga, including Hatha, Vinyasa, and Ashtanga. Whether you are a beginner or an accomplished yogi, you may find courses adapted to your requirements and tastes.

Meditation Retreats: Embark on a transforming journey of self-discovery by attending a meditation retreat on Koh Samui. These retreats provide organized programs that integrate diverse meditation approaches, mindfulness practices, and quiet contemplation. Participants may learn from expert meditation instructors and get insights into enhancing their meditation practice.

Beachside Yoga: Imagine practicing yoga on smooth sandy beaches with calm coastal breezes and the sound of waves lapping the shore. Koh Samui's oceanfront yoga classes give a unique and quiet experience. Whether it's a dawn or sunset yoga session, the natural beauty of the island enriches the practice, providing a greater feeling of relaxation and connection with nature.

9.3 Detox and Wellness Programs

Koh Samui is a famous location for detox and wellness programs intended at purifying the body and rejuvenating the mind. These programs provide a comprehensive approach to well-being, including specialized meals, cleaning treatments, exercise activities, and educational sessions.

Detox Retreats: Detoxification programs in Koh Samui concentrate on removing toxins from the body and enhancing general wellness. Guests may pick from several detox strategies, including juice fasting, raw food detox, or tailored cleansing diets. These retreats frequently feature daily yoga or fitness lessons, spa treatments, and educational lectures on healthy living.

health Workshops: Many health facilities and retreats in Koh Samui provide workshops and seminars on themes such as nutrition, mindfulness, stress management, and self-care. These training programs give vital insights and practical methods for sustaining a balanced and healthy lifestyle even after leaving the island.

exercise and Wellness Activities: Koh Samui's wellness programs frequently incorporate a variety of exercise activities to assist the detoxification process. These may include yoga, Pilates, water aerobics, beach exercises, and nature walks. Such exercises not only increase physical fitness but also add to general well-being and relaxation.

9.4 Traditional Thai Massages

No vacation to Koh Samui is complete without feeling the therapeutic touch of a traditional Thai massage. Rooted in ancient traditions and practices, Thai massage is recognized for its ability to ease muscular tension, enhance circulation, and promote general relaxation.

Thai Massage Techniques: Thai massage incorporates acupressure, deep stretching, and gentle rocking movements to increase the body's energy flow and relieve blockages. Therapists use their hands, elbows, knees, and feet to apply pressure to precise places along energy pathways, generating a feeling of balance and harmony.

Massage variants: In addition to basic Thai massage, numerous spas on the island provide variants and specialty treatments. These may include aromatherapy massages utilizing essential oils, herbal compress massages involving warm herbal pouches, and foot massages that target particular pressure areas on the feet.

Spa Rituals: Thai massages are sometimes part of a bigger spa ritual, integrating various treatments for a holistic health experience. Guests may luxuriate in exquisite packages that include body cleanses, facials, and soothing baths, giving a comprehensive pampering and rejuvenation experience.

9.5 Holistic Healing Techniques

Koh Samui is a site where traditional healing techniques and current holistic methods coexist. Visitors may experience a spectrum of alternative treatments and therapeutic practices, each having distinct advantages for physical, mental, and emotional well-being.

Reiki & Energy Healing: Experience the healing power of energy via Reiki and other energy-based treatments. Practitioners use global life force energy to restore balance and facilitate healing on a subtle level. These sessions are renowned to give profound relaxation, stress alleviation, and emotional release.

Traditional Chinese Medicine: Some health clinics in Koh Samui provide Traditional Chinese Medicine (TCM) therapies such as acupuncture, herbal medicine, and cupping therapy. TCM focuses on restoring the body's equilibrium and healing diseases by balancing the flow of Qi (energy) via meridians.

Sound Healing: Sound healing techniques employ the vibrations and frequencies of different instruments, such as singing bowls and gongs, to promote relaxation and equilibrium. The relaxing tones help relieve tension, decrease stress, and restore equilibrium to the mind and body.

Crystal Healing: Koh Samui's health facilities also offer crystal healing treatments, where crystals and gemstones are put on and around the body to balance energy and assist recovery. Each stone is considered to offer unique characteristics that may assist treat certain bodily, emotional, or spiritual difficulties.

Ayurveda: Experience the ancient knowledge of Ayurveda, an Indian holistic health approach.

Ayurvedic therapies, including massages, herbal cures, and tailored consultations, attempt to restore harmony and balance to the body, mind, and soul.

Koh Samui's health and spa retreats offer a refuge for relaxation, renewal, and self-discovery. Whether you seek physical treatment, mental serenity, or spiritual progress, the island's offers cater to varied health requirements, providing a genuinely transforming and unique experience.

Chapter 10: Shopping and Markets

Retail in Koh Samui is an exhilarating experience, giving a broad variety of alternatives from busy markets to contemporary retail complexes. This chapter will walk you through some of the top shopping spots on the island, including famous markets and places to buy unique local art and handicrafts.

10.1 Central Festival Samui

Central Festival Samui is the biggest and most popular retail mall on the island. Located in Chaweng, it is a contemporary complex that serves all retail requirements. With a large choice of foreign and local brands, this mall provides a comprehensive assortment of apparel, accessories, gadgets, and home products.

At Central Festival Samui, you'll discover well-known worldwide brands like Zara, H&M, and Adidas, as well as Thai designer shops and local handicraft stores. The mall also has a supermarket, a movie complex, and a range of restaurants and food courts providing both local and foreign cuisines. It's the ideal spot to spend a day indulging in retail therapy and having a meal or two.

10.2 Fisherman's Village Walking Street

Fisherman's Village Walking Street, situated in Bophut, is a busy night market that takes place every Friday evening. This market is notable for its unique combination of traditional and contemporary wares. As you meander through the small alleyways, you'll discover vendors offering a range of products, including apparel, accessories, handcrafted crafts, souvenirs, and artwork.

The market also has various food vendors where you may experience a broad selection of local specialties, from freshly grilled fish to traditional Thai sweets. Live music performances and cultural events contribute to the dynamic environment, giving a memorable experience for guests.

10.3 Lamai Night Market

Lamai Night Market, hosted every Sunday, is another must-visit shopping location on Koh Samui. Located in the village of Lamai, this market draws both residents and visitors searching for excellent discounts and a sense of local culture. The market comes alive in the evening with colorful vendors providing a range of things.

At Lamai Night Market, you'll discover a vast assortment of products such as apparel, accessories, handicrafts, gadgets, and souvenirs. The market is particularly renowned for its street food kiosks dishing up wonderful Thai meals and pleasant drinks. Don't miss the chance to eat some local foods like mango sticky rice and coconut pancakes while you tour the market.

10.4 Maenam Walking Street

Maenam Walking Street is a vibrant night market that takes place every Thursday in the town of Maenam. This market provides a more calm and laid-back ambiance compared to other of the bigger markets on the island. It is a terrific spot to browse for unique souvenirs and handicrafts manufactured by local craftsmen.

As you meander around Maenam Walking Street, you'll discover a broad assortment of merchandise including apparel, accessories, jewelry, home décor items, and handcrafted crafts. The market also contains food vendors selling a range of local delicacies and meals, making it a great spot to satiate your taste buds while shopping.

10.5 Local Art and Handicrafts

In addition to the lively markets, Koh Samui is noted for its indigenous art and handicrafts. Throughout the island, you'll find several art galleries, boutique stores, and workshops where you may discover unique artworks produced by brilliant local artists.

One popular spot for art fans is Bophut's Fisherman's Village, where you'll find various galleries showing modern art, traditional Thai paintings, and sculptures. These galleries regularly offer exhibits that showcase the work of local artists, giving a forum for creativity and cultural expression.

For those interested in traditional handicrafts, a visit to Nathon, the island's administrative hub, is suggested. Here, you may visit stores offering handcrafted textiles, pottery, wood carvings, and cutlery, all manufactured by local craftsmen. These original works make fantastic mementos or house decorations, displaying the rich creative tradition of Koh Samui.

Whether you're hunting for contemporary fashion goods, local souvenirs, or unique works of art, Koh Samui's retail scene offers something for everyone. From sophisticated malls to bustling markets and local art galleries, this chapter has offered a look into the many shopping experiences the island has to offer. So, be ready to buy until you drop and bring back treasured memories from your stay in Koh Samui.

Chapter 11: Dining and Cuisine

When it comes to gastronomic pleasures, Koh Samui provides a bustling and diversified eating scene that caters to all tastes and interests. Whether you're a lover of traditional Thai cuisine, seafood delights, foreign cuisines, or street food, or have a predilection for vegan and vegetarian choices, this chapter will lead you through the culinary marvels of the island.

11.1 Traditional Thai Food

Thai food is recognized worldwide for its powerful flavors, fragrant herbs, and harmonious balance of sweet, sour, spicy, and savory tastes. In Koh Samui, you'll have the chance to sample genuine Thai delicacies that represent the island's cultural past. From fiery Tom Yum Goong (hot and sour prawn soup) to creamy Massaman Curry, the tastes of Thailand will delight your taste buds. Be sure to taste famous meals like Pad Thai (stir-fried noodles), Som Tam (papaya salad), and Green Curry, which represent the rich and varied culinary traditions of the nation.

11.2 Seafood Specialties

With its seaside position, Koh Samui is heaven for seafood lovers. Fresh catches from the Gulf of Thailand are converted into exquisite meals that showcase the island's vast marine resources. Indulge in juicy grilled prawns, steamed fish with lime and chile, or aromatic seafood curries. For an amazing eating experience, travel to the local fish markets or seaside restaurants where you may select your seafood right from the tank and have it cooked to your preference.

11.3 International Cuisine

Koh Samui's eating scene extends beyond traditional Thai dishes, providing a broad choice of world cuisines to satisfy every appetite. From Italian trattorias to French bistros, and Japanese sushi bars to Indian curry restaurants, you'll discover a wealth of alternatives to fulfill your needs. Many restaurants are managed by competent foreign chefs who put their distinctive twists on traditional meals. Whether you're in the mood for a flawlessly cooked steak, a wood-fired pizza, or a dish of sushi rolls, Koh Samui offers a broad choice of foreign eating venues to pick from.

11.4 Street Food Experience

No visit to Thailand is complete without partaking in the colorful street food culture, and Koh Samui is no exception. Exploring the local street food scene looks like the original tastes and culinary traditions of the island. Wander through lively night markets and street stalls where you'll discover an assortment of delicious delicacies sizzling on hot grills and boiling in woks. Satay skewers, crunchy spring rolls, grilled sausages, and exotic fruit smoothies are just a few of the pleasures that await you. Don't miss out on sampling the iconic Thai street food staple, Pad Kra Pao (stir-fried minced pork with basil), which is sure to leave you hungry for more.

11.5 Vegan and Vegetarian Options

Koh Samui responds to the rising demand for vegan and vegetarian cuisine, making it a mecca for plant-based food connoisseurs. Many restaurants provide separate menus or have selections highlighted for people seeking meat-free alternatives. From healthful Buddha bowls and fresh salads to plant-based adaptations of traditional Thai cuisine, you'll discover a broad choice of savory and satisfying alternatives. The island also features vegan and vegetarian-friendly eateries and juice bars that serve up organic and locally produced products, offering a guilt-free and sustainable eating experience.

In Koh Samui, eating is not simply a source of sustenance but an experience that engages all your senses. From traditional Thai specialties to worldwide fusion cuisine, the island's eating choices are as varied as its guests. Whether you want to indulge in exquisite dining experiences, discover the local street food culture, or adopt a plant-based diet, Koh Samui guarantees to thrill your taste buds and create unique culinary memories.

Chapter 12: Nightlife and Entertainment

12.1 Chaweng Nightlife

Chaweng is the dynamic core of Koh Samui's nightlife culture, providing a varied choice of entertainment alternatives for night owls. The lively streets of Chaweng are dotted with pubs, clubs, and discos that cater to all interests and inclinations. Whether you're searching for a laid-back seaside pub or a high-energy dance club, Chaweng offers it all.

12.1.1 Beachfront Bars

One of the attractions of Chaweng's nightlife is the availability of beachside bars. These businesses provide a calm setting where you may sip a beverage while watching the waves softly wash against the coast. Popular seaside bars include Ark Bar, Coco Tams, and Bar Ice Samui. They generally offer live music, fire displays, and themed events, providing a vibrant and entertaining ambiance.

12.1.2 Nightclubs and Discos

For those wanting a more vibrant and uplifting nightlife experience, Chaweng is home to various nightclubs and discos. Places like Sound Club, Solo Bar, and Green Mango Club are renowned for their thumping music, state-of-the-art sound systems, and passionate DJs. These establishments draw both residents and visitors, creating a dynamic and varied party environment.

12.1.3 Pub Crawls and Bar Hopping

To make the most of Chaweng's nightlife, try joining a pub crawl or planning your own bar-hopping experience. This enables you to visit other pubs and clubs, meet new people, and enjoy the dynamic spirit of the town. Many tour firms provide pub crawl packages that include guided tours, cheap beverages, and VIP admission to prominent establishments.

12.2 Fisherman's Village Bars

Located in Bophut, Fisherman's Village provides a more laid-back and pleasant nightlife experience compared to Chaweng. This picturesque neighborhood is noted for its historic wooden houses, boutique stores, and a large assortment of taverns and restaurants.

12.2.1 Riverside Bars

One of the biggest attractions of Fisherman's Village is its riverbank taverns. These enterprises offer a lovely environment with views of the tranquil seas and fishing boats. Enjoy a refreshing drink at a riverbank pub like Coco Tam's, The Pier, or Karma Sutra, and immerse yourself in the calm environment of this quaint community.

12.2.2 Wine Bars and Cocktail Lounges

Fisherman's Village is also home to various wine bars and cocktail lounges, catering to those who seek a more sophisticated and polished nightlife experience. Sip on a bottle of quality wine or indulge in a handmade cocktail at venues like The Wine Bar Samui, The

Library, or The Shack. These places frequently provide a pleasant and private setting, excellent for relaxing after a long day of sightseeing.

12.2.3 Cultural Shows and Live Performances

In addition to its pubs, Fisherman's Village sometimes holds cultural exhibitions and live performances. Traditional Thai dance performances, fire displays, and live music are frequent attractions in this neighborhood. Keep an eye out for special events and performances, as they give you a unique chance to immerse yourself in the local culture while enjoying a night out.

12.3 Lamai Beach Nightclubs

Lamai Beach, situated on the southern shore of Koh Samui, is another famous nightlife location on the island. While not as hectic as Chaweng, Lamai provides a more relaxing and private ambiance with its assortment of nightclubs and pubs.

12.3.1 Music Bars and Lounges

Lamai Beach is renowned for its music bars and clubs, where you may enjoy live bands and acoustic performances. Relax in a nice atmosphere, listen to amazing performers, and sip on your favorite drink at venues like Shamrock Irish Pub, Samui Rock Bar, or Bondi Aussie Bar. These places frequently offer a cheerful and inviting ambiance, drawing both residents and visitors.

12.3.2 Night Markets and Beer Bars

Lamai also boasts night markets where you may experience the bustling environment while tasting local street cuisine and shopping through unique items. Beer pubs are sprinkled around the neighborhood, giving a more relaxed and cheap choice for a night out. Grab a cool drink, participate in pleasant discussions, and take up the colorful atmosphere of Lamai.

12.4 Cabaret Shows and Ladyboy Performances

Koh Samui is famed for its spectacular cabaret acts and ladyboy performances, and various places throughout the island provide these exciting spectacles. Witness the splendor, skill, and beautiful costumes of performers in establishments like Starz Cabaret, Paris Follies Cabaret, or Tiffany's Show Samui. These presentations are a memorable experience, exhibiting the distinct culture and variety of the island.

12.5 Live Music Venues

Throughout Koh Samui, you'll discover countless live music venues that cater to all genres and preferences. From reggae and rock to jazz and blues, there is something for everyone. Check out locations such as Coco Blues Bar, Frog, and Gecko, or Sweet Soul Café to hear excellent local and international artists playing in an intimate environment.

In conclusion, Koh Samui provides a bustling and diversified nightlife and entertainment scene. Whether you like the high-energy clubs of Chaweng, the lovely pubs of Fisherman's

Village, the relaxing environment of Lamai Beach, the glitz of cabaret shows, or live music performances, there are sufficient alternatives to suit your interests. Explore the many chapters in this book to, help you get the most out of your vacation to Koh Samui in 2023.

Chapter 13: Family-Friendly Activities

Family holidays are a fantastic chance to build lasting memories and establish ties. Koh Samui provides a broad choice of family-friendly activities that appeal to all age groups. Whether you're seeking exhilarating adventures or instructive encounters, this chapter will walk you through some of the greatest attractions suited for families.

13.1 Samui Aquarium and Tiger Zoo

Located in the south of Koh Samui, the Samui Aquarium and Tiger Zoo is a popular location for families wishing to discover the fascinating aquatic world and interact with gorgeous tigers. The aquarium shows an excellent assortment of tropical fish, colorful coral reefs, and uncommon aquatic critters. Visitors may see spectacular shark feedings and even swim with harmless reef sharks in a restricted area.

Adjacent to the aquarium, the Tiger Zoo gives a rare chance to come up close with these majestic big cats. Under the supervision of skilled trainers, families may see Bengal tigers, white tigers, and leopards as they wander inside wide enclosures. Educational exhibitions give insights into the lives and habits of these endangered animals, increasing awareness and conservation.

13.2 Coco Splash Water Park

For a fun-filled day under the sun, Coco Splash Water Park is a wonderful option. Located near Lamai Beach, this water park provides a selection of spectacular water slides, splash pools, and thrilling activities appropriate for all ages. Kids may enjoy mini-slides, water cannons, and small pools particularly intended for their safety and pleasure.

Meanwhile, older children and adults may enjoy the adrenaline thrill of high-speed slides, twisting tubes, and a lazy river. The park also has resting spaces with sun loungers, enabling parents to chill while keeping an eye on their small ones. With its tropical ambiance, Coco Splash Water Park offers a refreshing respite from the heat and promises a day of fun and excitement for the whole family.

13.3 Paradise Park Farm

Nestled in the center of Koh Samui's beautiful nature, Paradise Park Farm provides an immersive wildlife experience that mixes education and enjoyment. This family-friendly attraction shows a varied selection of exotic creatures, including monkeys, birds, reptiles, and more. Families may explore the park's expansive grounds on foot or opt for an entertaining guided tour.

The highlight of the Paradise Park Farm experience is the option to hand-feed animals such as deer, goats, and rabbits. Kids may engage with friendly monkeys, enjoy spectacular bird presentations, and learn about various species via educational displays and demonstrations. Additionally, the park provides spectacular panoramic views of the island, making it a great site for a family picnic or a ramble through nature.

13.4 Samui Monkey Theatre

Combining comedy, intellect, and entertainment, the Samui Monkey Theatre is a must-visit for families seeking a unique cultural experience. Located in the center of Koh Samui, this theater highlights the incredible abilities of native monkeys taught to perform engaging acts. These extremely adept monkeys are taught to ride bicycles, play musical instruments, and engage in amusing antics that will leave the whole family in wonder.

The shows not only entertain but also increase awareness about primate conservation and the need of protecting their natural habitats. Visitors may also engage with the monkeys after the presentation, allowing them an opportunity to observe their intellect up close and even snap unique pictures.

13.5 Samui Go Kart

For families with older children or teens searching for an adrenaline-packed experience, Samui Go Kart is a great option. Situated in Chaweng, this go-karting circuit provides an exciting experience for racing lovers of all skill levels. Families may compete against each other or just enjoy the rush of racing around the track in a safe and supervised setting.

The circuit gives numerous kart alternatives appropriate for various age groups, so that everyone may participate. Safety equipment, including helmets and training on kart operation, is supplied to provide a safe and fun experience. Samui Go Kart provides an action-packed day of friendly competition and thrill for the entire family.

Conclusion

Koh Samui provides a range of family-friendly activities that appeal to varied interests and age groups. From seeing aquatic life at the Samui Aquarium and Tiger Zoo to enjoying exhilarating water slides at Coco Splash Water Park, there are many chances for adventure and fun. Paradise Park Farm, Samui Monkey Theatre, and Samui Go Kart give unique experiences that blend entertainment, education, and cultural enrichment. These activities guarantee that families visiting Koh Samui will make amazing moments together, building a stronger connection and appreciation for the island's offers.

Chapter 14: Sustainable Tourism and Eco-friendly Practices

14.1 Responsible Tourism Initiatives

Responsible tourism is a rising movement that attempts to reduce the negative consequences of tourism on the environment and local people while enhancing the benefits. In Koh Samui, various responsible tourism programs have been launched to encourage sustainable habits among tourists and companies.

Tourists may contribute to responsible tourism by respecting the local culture and customs, protecting natural resources, and supporting local businesses. It's crucial to be careful of sensitive ecosystems, such as coral reefs and protected areas, and adopt safe snorkeling and diving methods to limit harm.

Local groups and tourist boards cooperate to increase awareness about responsible tourism via educational campaigns, seminars, and events. They urge people to participate in environmentally-friendly activities and support ethical wildlife interactions, such as visiting elephant sanctuaries that promote conservation and compassionate treatment of animals.

14.2 Eco-tours and Nature Conservation

Koh Samui provides a choice of eco-tours and environmental conservation programs that enable tourists to see the island's unique natural landscapes while supporting conservation efforts. These trips are meant to reduce environmental impact and encourage sustainable activities.

Eco-tours frequently involve guided treks into beautiful rainforests, where guests may learn about local flora and wildlife from expert guides. These trips concentrate on teaching people about the significance of conservation and conserving the island's biodiversity.

Another popular eco-friendly sport is kayaking or paddleboarding in the mangrove woods. This enables visitors to immerse themselves in the unique ecology while supporting its preservation. Many tour operators work closely with local conservation groups to ensure that these activities are handled properly and in harmony with nature.

Additionally, environmental conservation initiatives in Koh Samui employ volunteers in activities like beach cleanups, tree planting, and animal monitoring. These projects give possibilities for visitors to actively help to conserve the island's natural beauty.

14.3 Recycling and Waste Management

To address the environmental difficulties created by tourism, Koh Samui has established thorough recycling and trash management systems. Hotels, restaurants, and public areas have implemented recycling measures and urged tourists to contribute to decreasing garbage.

Recycling bins are strategically positioned across the island, making it easier for travelers to dispose of their garbage safely. Local authorities cooperate collaboratively with enterprises to encourage recycling methods, increase awareness about the necessity of trash reduction, and give training on effective waste management strategies.

Moreover, steps have been launched to limit single-use plastic usage. Many institutions have shifted to eco-friendly alternatives, such as biodegradable or reusable packaging. Visitors are asked to bring their reusable water bottles and shopping bags to prevent plastic waste.

By supporting these recycling and trash management activities, tourists can actively contribute to the preservation of Koh Samui's natural ecosystem and lessen the ecological imprint of tourism on the island.

14.4 Sustainable Accommodations

Sustainable lodgings are gaining popularity in Koh Samui as guests grow more concerned about their environmental effects. Many resorts and hotels have incorporated green techniques to lower their carbon impact and promote sustainability.

Sustainable lodgings emphasize energy efficiency by using renewable energy sources like solar power and applying energy-saving technology like LED lighting and sophisticated temperature control systems. They also include water-saving techniques, such as low-flow showerheads and toilets, and establish efficient wastewater management systems.

To limit waste, these lodgings frequently have recycling systems in place and eliminate single-use plastic by offering refillable toiletries and water dispensers. Some places even have organic gardens, where they obtain products for their restaurants, supporting local and organic produce.

When picking lodging, check for eco-certifications like Green Globe or Travelife, which show that the institution supports sustainable practices. Staying at sustainable lodgings not only enables travelers to enjoy a guilt-free holiday but also helps companies that promote environmental care.

14.5 Community-based Tourism Projects

Community-based tourism programs in Koh Samui give unique possibilities for tourists to connect with the local people, learn about their customs, and support their livelihoods. These programs attempt to generate a beneficial effect by encouraging cultural interchange and sustainable economic growth.

One example of community-based tourism is visiting local communities where tourists may experience traditional crafts and cultural performances. By buying locally manufactured handicrafts or participating in workshops, travelers directly support the local craftsmen and help preserve traditional workmanship.

Additionally, some programs provide homestays or village immersion experiences, enabling guests to stay with local families and experience their way of life. This personal engagement improves cultural awareness and gives immediate economic advantages to the community.

Participating in community-based tourism initiatives also aids local conservation efforts. For instance, some programs concentrate on turtle conservation, where visitors may learn about the necessity of safeguarding these endangered species and even assist in releasing hatchlings into the sea.

By participating in community-based tourism, tourists may have a meaningful and immersive experience while contributing to the socio-economic well-being of the local communities.

Overall, Chapter 14 underscores the necessity of sustainable tourism and eco-friendly measures in Koh Samui. Responsible tourism initiatives, eco-tours, recycling and trash management programs, sustainable lodgings, and community-based tourism projects all play a significant part in conserving the island's natural beauty and helping local communities. By adopting these behaviors and supporting these projects, tourists may assure a beneficial influence on the environment and help the long-term sustainability of tourism in Koh Samui.

Chapter 15: Safety and Health Tips

When traveling to Koh Samui, ensuring your safety and well-being should be a top priority. This chapter provides comprehensive information on various safety and health tips to help you have a worry-free and enjoyable trip.

15.1 Emergency Contact Information

It is crucial to be prepared for any unforeseen circumstances during your travels. Familiarize yourself with the emergency contact information for Koh Samui:

Emergency Services: In case of emergencies, dial 191 to reach the Thai emergency services, which include police, fire, and ambulance.
Tourist Police: The Tourist Police Hotline can be reached at 1155. They are specifically trained to assist tourists and can provide guidance and support in various situations.

Embassy or Consulate: Take note of the contact details for your country's embassy or consulate in Thailand. They can offer assistance in case of passport loss, legal matters, or other emergencies.

15.2 Medical Facilities and Pharmacies

Koh Samui offers a range of medical facilities and pharmacies to cater to travelers' healthcare needs. Here's what you need to know:

Hospitals: The main hospital on the island is Bangkok Hospital Samui, located in Chaweng. It provides comprehensive medical services, including emergency care and specialist treatments. Other hospitals like Samui International Hospital and Bandon International Hospital also offer quality healthcare services.

Clinics: Several clinics are available across the island, providing basic medical services, minor treatments, and consultations. These include Chaweng Clinic and Lamai Clinic, which are centrally located in popular tourist areas.

Pharmacies: Pharmacies are easily found in Koh Samui, and many medications are available over the counter. However, it is advisable to carry a sufficient supply of any prescription medications you require during your stay.

15.3 Sun Safety and Hydration

Koh Samui's tropical climate means ample sunshine, which requires precautions to protect yourself from the sun's harmful rays and stay hydrated. Follow these tips for sun safety and hydration:

Sunscreen: Apply a broad-spectrum sunscreen with a high SPF before heading out, even on cloudy days. Reapply every few hours, especially if you have been swimming or sweating.

Protective Clothing: Wear lightweight, breathable clothing that covers your skin, such as long sleeves and pants, to minimize direct sun exposure. A wide-brimmed hat and sunglasses also provide additional protection.

Hydration: Drink plenty of water throughout the day to stay hydrated in the heat. Carry a refillable water bottle and aim to consume at least 2-3 liters of water daily. Avoid excessive alcohol consumption, as it can contribute to dehydration.

Seek Shade: When the sun is at its peak (usually between 10 am and 4 pm), find shaded areas or take breaks indoors to avoid prolonged sun exposure.

15.4 Mosquito-borne Diseases

Being in a tropical destination like Koh Samui means encountering mosquitoes, which may carry diseases such as dengue fever and Zika virus. Take precautions to minimize the risk of mosquito bites:

Insect Repellent: Use a mosquito repellent containing DEET, picaridin, or oil of lemon eucalyptus on exposed skin. Apply it during the day and evening when mosquitoes are most active.

Protective Clothing: Wear long-sleeved shirts, long pants, and socks in the evening, especially if you are in outdoor areas with a high mosquito population.

Mosquito Nets: If your accommodation doesn't have screens or air conditioning, consider using mosquito nets while sleeping to create a protective barrier.

Eliminate Breeding Sites: Mosquitoes breed in stagnant water. Dispose of any standing water around your accommodation, such as in buckets or flower pots, to reduce the mosquito population.

15.5 Traveling with Children or Elderly

If you are traveling with children or elderly family members, it is essential to take additional precautions to ensure their safety and comfort:

Medical Considerations: Consult with your healthcare provider before the trip to address any specific health concerns or necessary vaccinations for children or elderly travelers.

Safety Measures: Keep a close eye on children and ensure they are supervised at all times, especially near water bodies and in crowded areas. Use child safety seats in vehicles if needed.

Accessibility: Consider the accessibility of your accommodation and attractions for elderly travelers. Look for accommodations with elevators or ground-floor rooms if mobility is a concern.

Medications and Supplies: Carry any necessary medications, medical supplies, or mobility aids required for children or elderly family members. Also, keep a copy of their medical records and emergency contact information with you.

By following these safety and health tips, you can enjoy a worry-free and memorable experience while exploring the beautiful island of Koh Samui. Remember to prioritize your well-being and take necessary precautions to ensure a safe and enjoyable trip for everyone involved.

Chapter 16: Local Customs and Etiquette

16.1 Respect for Thai Culture

Thailand is a country rich in traditions and customs, and visitors need to show respect for the local culture. Thai people greatly value politeness and harmony, and by understanding and adhering to their customs, you can have a more meaningful and enjoyable experience in Koh Samui. Here are some key aspects of respecting Thai culture:

Modesty: Thais appreciate modesty in both clothing and behavior. It is advisable to dress modestly, especially when visiting religious sites or rural areas. Avoid wearing revealing clothing, and be mindful of your actions to avoid offending local sensibilities.

Politeness: Thais place great emphasis on politeness and maintaining a calm demeanor. It is customary to greet people with a smile and the traditional Thai greeting, known as the "wai." The wai is performed by pressing your palms together in a prayer-like gesture and bowing slightly. It is a sign of respect and should be reciprocated.

Avoiding confrontations: Thais generally avoid confrontation and value harmonious interactions. It is important to remain calm and composed, even in challenging situations. Raising your voice or displaying anger is considered disrespectful and may cause a loss of face for both parties involved.

16.2 Dress Code and Temple Etiquette

Thailand is a predominantly Buddhist country, and temples hold significant cultural and religious importance. When visiting temples, it is essential to adhere to the dress code and observe proper etiquette. Here are some guidelines to follow:

Modest attire: Wear clothing that covers your shoulders, chest, and knees. Avoid wearing tank tops, shorts, or revealing outfits. Loose-fitting and lightweight clothing is appropriate, as it helps you stay cool in the tropical climate.

Removing shoes: Before entering a temple or someone's home, it is customary to remove your shoes. Look for a designated area or follow the locals' lead.

Respecting sacred areas: Temples often have areas that are considered sacred. These areas may be marked by signs or roped off. Be mindful of these boundaries and avoid entering restricted spaces unless instructed otherwise.

Observing silence: Temples are places of worship and meditation. Maintain a quiet and respectful demeanor inside the temple grounds. Refrain from using your mobile phone, speaking loudly, or engaging in disruptive behavior.

16.3 Greetings and Gestures

Thais have specific greetings and gestures that reflect their culture and show respect. Understanding and using these greetings can help you connect with the locals on a deeper level. Here are some common greetings and gestures:

Sawasdee: The word "Sawasdee" is used to say hello and goodbye in Thai. You can accompany it with a wai gesture to show respect.

Wai: The wai is a traditional Thai gesture used to greet others or show respect. It involves placing your palms together in a prayer-like position and bowing slightly. When greeting someone older or of higher social status, it is polite to initiate the wai.

Monks: When encountering Buddhist monks, show the utmost respect. Women should avoid direct physical contact with monks, and everyone should give them space and maintain a respectful distance.

Pointing with feet: It is considered impolite to point or gesture with your feet, as the feet are considered the lowest part of the body. Keep your feet on the ground and avoid pointing them toward people or sacred objects.

16.4 Tipping and Bargaining

Tipping and bargaining are common practices in Thailand, but they require some understanding of the local customs. Here are some tips to navigate these aspects of Thai culture:

Tipping: Tipping is not mandatory in Thailand, but it is appreciated for good service. In restaurants, a 10% service charge may already be added to the bill. If not, leaving a small tip is customary. For other services like taxis, hotel staff, or tour guides, rounding up the bill or giving a small tip is a kind gesture.

Bargaining: Bargaining is a common practice in local markets and smaller shops. However, it is not customary to bargain in large department stores or upscale establishments. When bargaining, do so with a smile and in a friendly manner. Remember that both parties should feel satisfied with the final agreed-upon price.

Polite refusal: If you are not interested in purchasing a product or service, it is polite to decline politely rather than engaging in aggressive bargaining or abruptly walking away.

16.5 Social Etiquette

Thai society has its own set of social etiquette that visitors should be aware of to ensure respectful interactions. Here are some key points to keep in mind:

Personal space: Thais value personal space and tend to stand or sit a bit farther apart compared to some Western cultures. Avoid invading someone's personal space unless invited to do so.

Public displays of affection: Thais are generally modest when it comes to public displays of affection. It is advisable to refrain from excessive displays of affection, such as kissing or hugging, in public places.

Feet and head: The feet are considered the lowest and dirtiest part of the body, while the head is considered the highest and most sacred. Avoid touching someone's head, and refrain from pointing or gesturing with your feet.

Respect for elders: Thai society places great respect on age and hierarchy. Show deference to elders and those in positions of authority. When seated in a group, it is customary to sit lower than older or more senior individuals.

By respecting local customs and adhering to Thai etiquette, you can immerse yourself in the local culture and show appreciation for the traditions and values of the people of Koh Samui.

Chapter 17: Language and Communication

17.1 Basic Thai Phrases

When visiting Koh Samui, it's generally beneficial to educate oneself with some basic Thai words. Although English is frequently spoken in tourist locations, residents appreciate the effort made to converse in their original language. Here are some basic Thai terms to improve your vacation experience:

"Hello" - "Sawasdee" (sah-wah-dee)
"Thank you" - "Khob khun" (kawb-koon)
"Yes" - "Chai" (chai)
"No" - "Mai chai" (mai-chai)
"Please" - "Ga-ru-na" (gah-roo-nah)
"Excuse me" - "Khor thot" (kawr-tot)
"Sorry" - "Khor thot" (kawr-tot)
"How much?" - "Tao rai?" (tao-rai)
"Where is...?" - "Yoo nai...?" (yoo-nai)
"I don't understand" - "Mai kao jai" (mai-kao-jai)
"Goodbye" - "La gon" (la-gon)

17.2 English Proficiency

English proficiency in Koh Samui varies among residents. In important tourist sites and institutions, you'll discover many individuals who can speak and comprehend English. However, in more isolated or rural locations, the level of English may be restricted. It's a good idea to learn a few Thai words or carry a translation tool to overcome any communication gaps.

Hotels, resorts, restaurants, and tour operators frequently have English-speaking staff members who can help you. It's vital to explain critical information, such as dietary limitations or medical concerns, properly to guarantee comprehension.

17.3 Language Tips for Travelers

To improve your conversation easier and more productive, try these linguistic tips:

Learn fundamental greetings and phrases: Show respect and kindness by learning basic

Thai greetings and phrases. Locals will appreciate your effort and may be more likely to help you.

Use basic language: Speak slowly and clearly while engaging with natives who have weak English abilities. Use basic terminology and avoid complicated sentence patterns.

Non-verbal communication: Remember that communication is not simply about words. Pay attention to non-verbal signs, such as gestures, facial expressions, and body language. Be attentive to your non-verbal clues to guarantee clarity in your message.

Be patient and polite: Thai culture puts tremendous significance on politeness and patience. Stay cool and controlled, especially if there are communication challenges. A grin and a welcoming attitude may go a long way in building a favorable relationship.

Carry a phrasebook or translation software: Having a phrasebook or a language translation program on your smartphone may be quite useful when you face language problems. It enables you to easily check translations or even display the translated content to the person you're chatting with.

17.4 Language Apps and Resources

In today's digital era, various language applications and tools are available to aid tourists in overcoming language obstacles. Here are a few common options:

Google Translate: This program enables you to input or speak a sentence, and it gives a translation in real-time. It also features a camera translation tool, which might be beneficial for reading signage or menus.

iTranslate: iTranslate is another helpful translation program that supports various languages. It features voice recognition and offline translation capabilities.

Thai Phrasebook and Dictionary applications: There are various applications particularly developed to assist tourists learn and speak

Thai. They give phrase collections, pronunciation guidelines, and offline accessibility.

Language Learning Platforms: Platforms like Duolingo and Rosetta Stone provide Thai language courses, enabling you to study at your speed before your trip. They typically feature interactive tasks and quizzes to improve your learning experience.

17.5   Cultural   Sensitivity   in Communication

When talking with natives in Koh Samui, it's crucial to be culturally respectful. Here are some ideas to bear in mind:

Use the Wai gesture: The Wai is a traditional Thai greeting where palms are put together in a prayer-like motion. It's a symbol of respect and should be returned when welcomed by natives.

Address people respectfully: Use suitable titles when addressing persons. "Khun" is a courteous way to address someone, regardless of their gender. For example, "Khun Somchai" or "Khun Mrs. Smith."

Mind your body language: In Thai culture, it's crucial to avoid pointing with your foot or touching someone's head, since these behaviors are considered rude. Maintain a comfortable and courteous stance throughout discussions.

Be careful of personal space: Thai people appreciate personal space, so be mindful of keeping a suitable distance during interactions. Adjust your closeness depending on the comfort level of the person you're communicating with.

Adapt to the Thai idea of "sanuk": "Sanuk" refers to the Thai notion of having fun and enjoying oneself. Incorporate a lighter and cheery tone while talking, since Thais like comedy and positivism.

By being courteous, tolerant, and open-minded, you'll cultivate great encounters and create unforgettable experiences throughout your stay in Koh Samui.

Chapter 18: Koh Samui Festivals & Events

Koh Samui is not merely a tropical paradise noted for its gorgeous beaches and crystal-clear seas. It is also a bustling location that stages several festivals and events throughout the year, exhibiting the rich cultural legacy and different entertainment alternatives available on the island. This chapter highlights some of the most notable festivals and events that take place on Koh Samui, enabling visitors to immerse themselves in the local culture and create amazing experiences.

18.1 Songkran Water Festival

One of the most thrilling and highly celebrated celebrations in Thailand is the Songkran Water Festival, honoring the traditional Thai New Year. Taking place in mid-April, this event is noted for its vigorous water battles and cheerful festivities. Koh Samui comes alive at this time, with residents and visitors alike flocking to the streets equipped with water pistols and buckets, engaged in friendly water wars to represent washing away the previous year's woes. The event also involves visits to temples, giving prayers, and making merit. Tourists may participate in the celebrations, throwing water on bystanders and relishing in traditional Thai dishes.

18.2 Loy Krathong Festival

The Loy Krathong Festival, sometimes known as the Festival of Lights, is another prominent festival observed in Koh Samui. Usually conducted in November, this charming celebration includes floating tiny, adorned baskets made of banana leaves, flowers, and candles across rivers, lakes, and the sea. These lit krathongs are cast adrift to pay honor to the water goddess and to remove any bad energy or regrets. Visitors may participate in the celebrations by building their krathongs and joining the locals in the hypnotic sight of hundreds of flashing lights brightening the night.

18.3 Samui Regatta

For sailing fans and sports lovers, the Samui Regatta is an event not to be missed. Held annually in May, this globally regarded sailing tournament draws sailors from across the globe. The event shows the beauty of Koh Samui's shoreline and provides exhilarating racing in many categories. Visitors may watch the amazing sight of beautiful yachts skimming through the blue waves while enjoying the vibrant atmosphere and cheering on the contestants. The Samui Regatta is a terrific chance to enjoy the excitement of competitive sailing and see the island's natural grandeur.

18.4 Ten Stars Samui Art Party

For art fans and creative individuals, the Ten Stars Samui Art Party gives a unique platform to admire and connect with the local art scene. This event, generally held in July, brings together brilliant painters, photographers, sculptors, and performers to present their works in a bright and participatory atmosphere. Visitors may explore art exhibits, watch live painting sessions, and even engage in seminars to master different creative skills. The Ten Stars Samui Art Party develops a feeling of community and respect for the arts, making it a must-visit event for people seeking cultural enrichment.

18.5 International Jazz Festival

Music fans visiting Koh Samui should arrange their vacation to coincide with the International Jazz Festival, a spectacular event that celebrates the beautiful melodies of jazz. Typically held in February, this event gathers famous jazz performers from throughout the globe, producing an exhilarating environment. Visitors may enjoy enthralling concerts by skilled performers, ranging from classic jazz to current fusion. The event also incorporates seminars, jam sessions, and late-night performances at different locations around the island. The International Jazz Festival delivers amazing musical experiences against the background of Koh Samui's magnificent nature.

These festivals and events in Koh Samui not only give amusement but also provide a better knowledge of the island's customs, cultural history, and creative accomplishments. Whether it's engaging in water fights during Songkran, floating krathongs under the moonlight, witnessing exhilarating yacht races, immersing in the art scene, or grooving to the smooth tunes of jazz, these experiences allow travelers to create lasting memories and forge connections with the local community. Koh Samui's festivals and events exhibit the island's colorful character and allow visitors a chance to enjoy life in this tropical paradise.

Chapter 19: Beyond Koh Samui

19.1 Exploring surrounding islands: Koh Phangan, Koh Tao

Koh Samui is not the only jewel in the Gulf of Thailand. The area is home to two additional gorgeous islands, Koh Phangan and Koh Tao, each with its distinct charms and charm. Exploring these adjacent islands might offer a whole new depth to your tropical experience.

19.1.1 Koh Phangan: Famous for its Full Moon

Party and magnificent beaches, Koh Phangan is only a short boat ride away from Koh Samui. While the Full Moon Party is surely a highlight for many tourists, there is much more to see on the island. Head to Thong Nai Pan Noi or Thong Nai Pan Yai, two stunning beaches in the northeast, where you may relax on the silky white sand and swim in crystal-clear waters. Don't miss the opportunity to explore the Phaeng Waterfall, a breathtaking cascade surrounded by thick vegetation. If you're wanting a more calm experience, visit the island's quieter west coast with beaches like Haad Salad and Haad Yao. Koh Phangan also provides superb diving and snorkeling options, with vivid coral reefs teaming with marine life.

19.1.2 Koh Tao: Known as the "Turtle Island,"

Koh Tao is a haven for divers and snorkelers. This little island is recognized for its clean seas, vivid coral reefs, and complex marine ecology. Explore the undersea world by going on a diving tour, where you may see beautiful tropical fish, sea turtles, and even whale sharks. If you're new to diving, Koh Tao is a fantastic spot to become certified, since there are multiple dive schools providing lessons for different levels. Sairee Beach, the island's major center, is packed with lively restaurants, bars, and boutiques, catering to both divers and beach lovers. For a stunning perspective, trek up to the John-Suwan Viewpoint, where you can take in panoramic panoramas of the island and its surrounding seas.

19.2 Day excursions to Surat Thani and Ang Thong

If you're interested in seeing the mainland and its adjacent attractions, try taking day excursions to Surat Thani and Ang Thong.

19.2.1 Surat Thani

Situated on the mainland, Surat Thani is a busy provincial capital and a gateway to the southern area of Thailand. The city looks at true Thai culture and everyday life. Visit the bustling Talad Tawad Night Market, where you can sample a variety of local foods and purchase gifts. Don't miss the opportunity to tour the Chaiya National Museum, which highlights the area's rich history and historical relics. For nature enthusiasts, a vacation to Khao Sok National Park is highly recommended. Immerse yourself in the lush rainforest, embark on a guided jungle hike, or enjoy a breathtaking boat ride on Cheow Lan Lake, flanked by towering limestone cliffs.

19.2.2 Ang Thong National Marine Park

Located off the west coast of Koh Samui, Ang Thong National Marine Park is a beautiful archipelago consisting of 42 islands. The park is recognized for its magnificent scenery, including towering limestone karsts, quiet beaches, and emerald-green lagoons. Join a guided trip to see the park's attractions, including the breathtaking perspective at Koh Wua Talap, the secret lagoon of Mae Koh Island, and the brilliant coral reefs around Koh Sam Sao. You may also kayak through the park's small rivers, exploring secret caverns and fascinating rock formations. Overnight camping excursions are provided for those who prefer to appreciate the park's grandeur beneath a starry sky.

19.3 Southern Thailand Excursions

If you have more time and wish to explore farther south, try visiting other sites in southern Thailand.

19.3.1 Krabi

Known for its stunning limestone cliffs, clean beaches, and clear turquoise seas, Krabi is a favorite destination for nature enthusiasts and adventure seekers. Take a long-tail boat to Railay Beach, a haven for rock climbers, or visit the famed Phi Phi Islands, featured in the movie "The Beach." Explore the Thung Teao Forest Natural Park and swim in the crystal-clear Emerald Pool. Krabi is also a good base for island hopping, with possibilities to explore adjacent islands like Koh Lanta, Koh Phi Phi Don, and Koh Hong.

19.3.2 Phuket

As Thailand's biggest island, Phuket provides a broad selection of sights and activities. Explore the exciting nightlife of Patong Beach, wander through the ancient alleyways of Old Phuket Town, or rest on the calm beaches of Kata and Karon. Take a boat journey to the famed James Bond Island, noted for its unusual limestone rock structure, or explore the adjacent Phi Phi Islands for magnificent snorkeling and diving opportunities. Phuket also features magnificent resorts, world-class golf courses, and a range of shopping and eating alternatives.

19.4 Bangkok and Northern Thailand Extension

For a comprehensive Thailand experience, consider extending your vacation to Bangkok and seeing the cultural and natural attractions of northern Thailand.

19.4.1 Bangkok

Thailand's busy capital is a city of contrasts, where ancient temples stand alongside contemporary skyscrapers. Visit the magnificent Grand Palace and Wat Phra Kaew, home of the venerated Emerald Buddha. Explore the bustling marketplaces of Chatuchak and Damnoen Saduak, where you can immerse yourself in the local culture and eat wonderful street cuisine. Take a boat trip down the Chao Phraya River, explore the floating markets, and experience the city's lively nightlife. Bangkok also provides a broad choice of housing alternatives, from budget-friendly guesthouses to luxury hotels.

19.4.2 Northern Thailand

Escape the tropical heat and go to the cooler areas of northern Thailand. Chiang Mai, the cultural capital, is noted for its historic temples, traditional markets, and the yearly Yi Peng Lantern Festival. Explore the Doi Suthep Temple, set on a hilltop above the city, or visit the Elephant Nature Park, where you may engage with rescued elephants responsibly. Take a vacation to Pai, a laid-back town surrounded by magnificent mountains and waterfalls, or go hiking in the lush forests of Chiang Rai, home of the famed White Temple (Wat Rong Khun).

19.5 Tips for Island Hopping

When beginning island-hopping expeditions, it's vital to keep a few guidelines in mind:

19.5.1 investigate and plan

Before going out on your island hopping adventure, investigate the islands you desire to visit, their transportation choices, and the activities they offer. Plan your schedule appropriately to make the most of your time.

19.5.2 Check boat timetables

Be careful to check the ferry or boat schedules between the islands to ensure a seamless changeover. It's essential to purchase your tickets in advance, particularly during high travel seasons.

19.5.3 Pack basics

Carry essentials such as sunscreen, bug repellant, a hat, and a reusable water bottle. It's also advisable to take a waterproof bag to preserve your stuff during boat journeys.

19.5.4 Respect nature and local culture

While touring the islands, be careful of the environment and adhere to responsible travel practices. Respect the local culture and traditions, and observe any recommendations offered by tour companies or national parks.

19.5.5 remain hydrated and pack snacks

Island hopping may be exhausting, so it's crucial to remain hydrated and energetic. Carry a water bottle and some snacks to keep you fuelled throughout the day.

By traveling beyond Koh Samui, you'll discover the various beauty of the Gulf of Thailand and enjoy the rich culture and natural marvels of southern Thailand. Whether you want to visit local islands, take day trips to mainland sites, or extend your tour to Bangkok and northern Thailand, these excursions will improve your travel experience and create memorable memories.

Chapter 20: Traveling Responsibly: Leaving a Positive Impact

In Chapter 20 of the "Koh Samui (Thailand) Travel Guide 2023," we address the significance of visiting ethically and leaving a good impression on the location. As responsible tourists, we have to safeguard the environment, help local communities, and encourage sustainable practices. This chapter includes ideas and recommendations on how you may make a difference during your vacation to Koh Samui.

20.1 Reduce, Reuse, and Recycle

One of the core concepts of sustainable travel is to avoid waste and lower our carbon footprint. Koh Samui, like many other tourist sites, confronts issues relating to garbage management. As a responsible tourist, you may contribute to a cleaner environment by adopting the following practices:

Reduce: Bring a reusable water bottle, shopping bag, and toiletries to limit single-use plastic waste. Choose eco-friendly items and avoid superfluous packaging.

Reuse: Opt for reusable things wherever practical, such as refillable toiletry containers, bamboo utensils, and cloth napkins. Use rechargeable batteries for your gadgets.

Recycle: Familiarize yourself with the local recycling facilities and sort your garbage correctly. Many hotels and resorts in Koh Samui have recycling programs in place, making it simpler for you to dispose of recyclable goods.

By implementing these principles into your everyday routine, you may drastically lessen your influence on the environment and help keep Koh Samui clean and attractive.

20.2 Supporting Local Businesses

Supporting local businesses is an important component of ethical travel. By choosing to visit locally owned enterprises, you contribute to the local economy and help maintain the distinct cultural history of Koh Samui. Here are some ways you may help local businesses:

Accommodation: Opt for locally owned hotels, resorts, or guesthouses instead of foreign chains. This enables your purchases to directly assist the local community.

Dining: Seek eateries and food carts that provide genuine Thai cuisine produced from locally available ingredients. By eating at these places, you support local farmers and help the preservation of traditional culinary methods.

Shopping: Explore local markets and stores to buy souvenirs, handicrafts, and locally created items. This helps maintain local artists and craftspeople, ensuring their talents and traditions are handed down to future generations.

Tours & Excursions: Choose tour operators and guides that have a strong commitment to sustainability and ethical tourism practices. Look for operators that encourage cultural understanding, care for the environment, and contribute to the local community.

Remember, by supporting local businesses, you not only contribute to the local economy but also develop genuine ties with the people of Koh Samui.

20.3 Volunteering and Community Engagement

Volunteering and community involvement provide chances to give back to the local community and have a positive effect on your travels. Koh Samui offers several programs and organizations that seek volunteers. Consider the following activities:

Beach Cleanups: Participate in scheduled beach cleanups to help preserve the island's gorgeous beaches free of rubbish. Check with local environmental groups or your hotel for forthcoming clean-up efforts.

Conservation Projects: Join local conservation programs focusing on safeguarding marine life, coral reefs, or maintaining natural environments. These initiatives typically give education and hands-on experiences, enabling you to contribute to the long-term sustainability of Koh Samui's ecology.

Community Outreach: Engage with local communities through volunteering at schools, orphanages, or community centers. Share your skills and experience with locals, engage in cultural exchanges or aid with local development initiatives.

Volunteering not only allows having a good influence but also provides a greater knowledge of the local culture and difficulties faced by the community.

20.4   Conservation   and   Wildlife Protection

Koh Samui is home to varied habitats, including tropical rainforests, mangroves, and marine regions. Preserving these natural areas and conserving the local fauna is crucial for maintaining the ecological balance. Here are some ways you may help conservation efforts:

Responsible Wildlife Interactions: Choose ethical wildlife encounters that promote animal well-being. Avoid activities that involve confined animals, such as elephant riding, or acts that exploit animals for amusement. Instead, support respected sanctuaries that prioritize rehabilitation and conservation.

Marine Conservation: Practice appropriate snorkeling and diving by respecting marine life and coral reefs. Avoid touching or treading on corals, and never feed or pursue marine creatures. Choose operators that follow sustainable diving methods and advocate reef protection.

Nature routes & Hiking: Stay on authorized routes and follow recommendations to avoid disruption to plant and animal life. Avoid littering and comply with any restrictions or instructions offered by the national parks or nature reserves.

By being attentive to your activities and supporting conservation projects, you help the long-term preservation of Koh Samui's natural beauty.

20.5 Inspiring Others to Travel Responsibly

As a responsible traveler, you have the potential to inspire others and encourage sustainable behaviors. Share your experiences and information with other travelers, friends, and family. Here are some ways you may support responsible travel:

Social Media Influence: Use your social media networks to promote responsible travel behaviors and highlight sustainable efforts in Koh Samui. Share advice, photographs, and experiences that urge people to be conscious of their influence on the environment and local communities.

Travel Blogging: Start a travel blog or contribute to existing platforms to share your ethical travel experiences. Provide ideas on eco-friendly lodgings, sustainable activities, and how tourists may have a good effect.

Engage in debates: Join online travel groups and forums to engage in debates about responsible travel. Share your experiences, learn from others, and create awareness about the necessity of sustainable tourism.

By sharing the message of responsible tourism, you may inspire a collaborative effort to conserve Koh Samui's natural and cultural legacy for decades to come.

In conclusion, traveling properly is vital for protecting the beauty and sustainability of Koh Samui. By adopting activities like avoiding trash, supporting local businesses, volunteering, encouraging conservation, and inspiring others, you may leave a beneficial impression on the destination. Remember, simple acts may make a major impact, and together we can assure a better future for Koh Samui and other vacation destinations throughout the globe.

Printed in Great Britain
by Amazon

39493141R00089